TH

ITALIAN

Catholic Divorce

Annette C. Schiro

Table of Contents

Front Lt to Rt: Giuseppe Nastasi, Antonia Nastasi

Back row Lt to Rt, sons Giuseppe (Joseph), Fillipo (Philip)

Dedication

To Our Lady of the Snows

I dedicate this book to the memory of my mother, Antoinette Nastasi Schiro, for her influence, inspiration, and whose stories are forever imprinted on my heart.

Also, this dedication would not be complete without giving glory to God for His divine inspiration and permission for Our Lady of the Snows to make guest appearances in my life.

The Italian Catholic Divorce

In the mid 1800's and early 1900's, a lot of Sicilians emigrated from Sicily to the United States. Some of them came into the port of New Orleans. This is where my ancestors got off the boat, and settled near New Orleans. My mother said that her family wanted to come to America because they heard that the streets were paved with gold.

My mother's paternal grandmother, Antonia Nastasi, came over with her husband, Giuseppe, and their six children in the early 1900's. It was a hasty departure from Italy as my mother told me. Apparently, Antonia and her husband were in a tavern, when she looked across the room and saw a woman flirting with Giuseppe. She promptly went over to the fireplace, picked up a fire iron, and proceeded to "go take care of that". It ended tragically for the flirtatious woman, and Antonia and her family took the first boat out of Italy.

Antonia had borne her first child, Libonio, before she was thirteen years of age. However, it was another 13 years before she had her next child. No one really knows when she got married to her husband Giuseppe, or even if he was the father of her first child. By the time she made her departure from Italy, she had had six children in all. My mother said that she really didn't like her grandmother

Antonia, and that she wasn't a very nice lady. When my mother was born at home in Bogalusa, Louisiana, Antonia ran down to city hall and had it recorded that her name was Antonia, naming my mother after herself, before my mom's own mother had a chance to name her. My mother later changed her name to Antoinette.

About the same time Antonia and her family came to America, Antonia's sister's husband, Roy Monteleone, also came over to make his fortune. He was supposed to save up enough money to send for his wife, Vita, and their daughters Katie and Rosa, back in Italy. Roy was so busy spending his money on drinking and wild women that he never sent money to his wife in Italy. Antonia decided that if she saved up enough money for her sister to come over, that Roy would straighten up once she got here. So they got all the money together and sent for Vita and her daughters. However, when they arrived, Roy didn't change his ways, and still spent his money on booze and wild women.

Back in those days she couldn't get a divorce because our family was Catholic, and Catholics could not divorce, because if you did, you would be excommunicated from the church, and bring disgrace on the whole family. The only way for her to marry again, was if her husband died. Enter the Italian Catholic Divorce. My great grandmother Antonia, who was already thrown out of one country for murder, decided against taking care of this matter herself, and sent her son Fillipo to "go take care of that", as my mother put it. So he did. And Antonia's sister went off and remarried. Of course Fillipo spent the next couple of years in jail, but it was only a slap on the wrist because, of course, it was self-defense. At least that's what he said. I often joke to my husband that we will never get divorced, and if he doesn't behave I will call my uncle Guy to "go take care of that".

The Arrangement

"I'll take him, but I won't take him!" exclaimed my grandmother Josephine. It was an acceptable arrangement to all the parties involved, and the date was set. On June 30, 1917, Josephine Gagliano (pronounced Gal-yee-ano) was wed to Joseph Nastasi. She was 15 years old, and Joseph was 21.

It all started when her father decided that she should get married. My mother said that Josephine and her father, Gaetano, did not get along very well, and he was looking to get rid of her. He needed sons to work the farm, and girls were considered more of a liability. They had never bothered to educate her, so she never learned to read or write.

Josephine's parents, Gaetano and Rosa Gagliano, were tenant farmers in Louisiana. They rented land from Antonio Nastasi, son of the infamous Antonia Nastasi. Antonio and his wife also had a grocery store and oyster bar in Independence, Louisiana. It was through Antonio that Gaetano met Antonia Nastasi. Antonia apparently wanted to marry off her son Fillipo, who was only 17 at the time. Antonia and Gaetano made an agreement that Antonia's son Fillipo would marry Josephine. All the families involved were immigrants and still carried on as if they were in the old country; they still spoke Italian, still practiced the traditions of the old country, and still arranged marriages.

On the appointed day, when Fillipo was supposed to go meet the girl he was to marry, he was so nervous that he asked his older brother Joseph to accompany him. When Josephine was presented with her husband to be, she took one look at his brother Joseph, and promptly declined to marry Fillipo, and agreed to marry Joseph. It really was love at first sight.

After Fillipo was rejected by his "would be" wife, Josephine, he sought to find his own match in the daughter of Roy Monteleone. On January 30, 1918, Fillipo's 18th birthday, Fillipo ran off to New Orleans and eloped with 15 year old Rosa Monteleone. Her mother, Vita, happened to be sisters with his own mother, Antonia. Rosa and Fillipo's marriage was pretty happy despite the fact that sometime in the 1930's, Fillipo had to go on a long business trip to "go take care of something" for his mother. Meanwhile his wife and children moved to Savannah, Georgia to await his return.

Nonno

Nonno: noun, the father of one's father or mother.

My dad's father, Joseph (Joe) Schiro, was around twelve years old when he made the voyage from Sicily to America. He made the trip along with his mother Maria, and sister Rosalia. His father Giorgio had left Pianna de Greggia, Sicily, to come to America five years before, around 1890. Giorgio had been working on a sugarcane plantation near Donaldsonville, Louisiana, to save up enough money to send to his family for their voyage to America.

Joe and his family were really lucky, because some men came to America, but were never heard from again. Railroads, plantations, and other industries needed laborers, and agents were paid commissions to get immigrants to come to America. They touted America as the Promised Land. They painted a picture of wealth and opportunity to get people to come here. Most men that came to America thought that they would return to their families as wealthy men.

Many of the poor peasant farmers that came here, ended up as poor tenant farmers here in the U.S. Conditions didn't seem to be much better than they were back at home. Maybe it was the shame of failure, or maybe they ended up starving and homeless. Whatever the reason, many wives and children were left abandoned back in Italy.

My grandfather, Joe, never forgot his voyage to America. He said the passengers were herded like animals onto the ships. There were no staterooms, and instead they were all crowded into one big room. It was not uncommon for these ships to carry several hundred people at a time. The more passengers they brought to America, the more money the captain and the ship would be paid. There were no sanitation measures taken, and the cabinets that they used to store human wastes would spill all over the floors in rough seas. Consequently, there was a high rate of sickness and disease. Many people died during the voyage that lasted almost two weeks.

When Joe and his family finally arrived at the port of New Orleans, there was a plague of yellow fever in the city. The ship wasn't allowed to dock unless the captain accepted a 30 day quarantine. The captain refused to be quarantined, and instead sailed the ship up into the inland waters to Plarfumine, Louisiana. The people were allowed to get off the boat after the mayor of the town had sponsored the ship.

Joe and his family took a ferry across the river to the Burnside plantation to meet his father. They remained there for five years. When Joe was 17 years old, he went to Roscoe, Illinois, to work on the railroad as a water boy, but he returned to his parents after six months.

His family finally settled in a village called Popular Grove, where Joe met his wife, Virginia, and they were married in September of 1911. Soon after, Joe's dad bought a farm in Lobdell, Louisiana, and the whole family moved there. The village had one general store that was also a post office. My father, Giorgio, was born in December of 1912, and by 1917, Virginia had had four children in all.

The family grew various crops, but the farm was always poor. My father, being the oldest, always had to help out on the farm. They grew sugarcane, and when it was harvest time, Nonno Joe went to get my dad out of school to come home and chop sugar cane. This is why my father only finished school up to the sixth grade.

Eventually my father moved to Rockford, Illinois in the 1930's to seek employment, and the whole family soon followed. My father got a job at the General Electric Radio Factory where he met my mother.

The American dream seemed to end up paying off for my parents and their families. They worked hard and did well, especially when the economy was good. If my ancestors would have stayed in Italy, they might still be poor peasant farmers today.

In all, I have traveled to enough foreign countries, including Italy, to know that here in America we are truly blessed: from spacious houses with indoor plumbing, to soft, plush toilet paper. No other country has afforded its people with the opportunities and luxuries that America has. It truly was the land of opportunity.

Joseph & Virginia Schiro

She Doesn't Speak Italian

I like to tell stories. When I'm involved in a conversation, or someone asks me a question, I can't always reply with a short answer. Sometimes, I have to tell a short story to get my point across. I come by it honestly; my mother, Antoinette, was a storyteller. In her later years, I would go to her house and sit on the couch, and she would tell me stories of her family, and share memories she had of when she was a little girl. Some of these stories revealed many skeletons in our family closet that she had been keeping quiet about for a long time. She probably decided that because all the parties involved were now deceased, there is no point in staying silent. She came by some of these stories somewhat dishonestly.

Sometime in 1923, my mother and her family moved to Rockford, Illinois, from Louisiana, when she was about four years old. They settled in the Italian section of town where a lot of Sicilians lived, and they all spoke the language of the old country. It was in the neighborhood of the famous Maria's Italian Restaurant. Maria started the restaurant in the back of her family's grocery store. It became so popular that they needed more space, so they moved it across the street, where it remained for over 80 years. When the family finally decided to close it down, it was still a popular restaurant, a landmark for every Italian that had come to settle in Rockford. My mother remembered walking down the sidewalk and passing by Maria's window, where the smell of the simmering spaghetti sauce would tease her appetite. I remember eating at Maria's as a child, and as an adult, it was always the same story; we had reservations, we would arrive there, and then be told to "wait in the bar" which could last as long as an hour or more. I quit eating there because we could never get a table. I think you had to be a regular, or famous to get a seat. Maria's closed down in 2013 after 90 years of business.

All the Italian ladies used to gather together to gossip. This was a regular pastime, since there was no such thing as a TV for entertainment back then. It was a rather common practice to gather in the middle of the street and stand there to talk. "Occasionally", my mother said, "there was a cat fight in the middle of the street". When the women got together to talk, they would always speak to each other in Italian.

It was real common for parents to not teach their children Italian, because they wanted their children to be American, and fit into the American society. They sent them to American schools where they were required to learn and speak only English. Also, the adults could speak to each other in Italian, and the children would not know what was being said. It was their secret language, or so they thought. Children pick up language just by listening. It happens in every language. Parents say things they think the children are too small to understand, only to find out different, when the child starts repeating things the parents wish they had never said. Everyone around my mother spoke Italian, her parents spoke Italian, her grandparents spoke Italian, the entire neighborhood spoke Italian, but since she would only reply in English, they never realized that she understood the language.

One day, my mother's mother, Josephine, had a bunch of the Italian ladies over for coffee and a gossip session. As the ladies were huddled around the table, engaged in telling stories of adultery, vice, and murder, my mother was in the corner of the room playing quietly with her dolls as inconspicuously as possible. At one point, one of the ladies nodded her head in the direction of my mother, and said in Italian, "What about her? She's listening to everything we say." To which Josephine replied, "It's ok, she doesn't speak Italian".

The Egg

Since my mother grew up in the 1920's and '30's, her family had to struggle through the great depression. Money was tight, and food was rationed out to all the family members. Her mother would put a pot of something on the stove, and it would simmer all day long, and when a meal time came, it was ready and waiting on the stove. It didn't matter if it was breakfast, lunch, or dinner, that's what there was to eat that day. They ate the same thing at every meal. There was no such thing as a different food for every meal. Sometimes, it was a pot of beans, other times it was a pot of vegetable soup. If they were lucky, the soup would have some meat in it, but it was mostly the adults that got to eat the meat. If times were good, the children might also get a piece.

My mother's father, Joseph, liked to raise chickens. However, they never ate them because they were his pets. When her dad wanted chicken to eat, her mom would have to go the store and buy one. My mother complained that she always ended up with the neck of the chicken. Joseph had a chicken coop for the hens to lay eggs, and apparently it was ok if they ate the eggs.

One day between meals my mother got so hungry, that she went outside to the chicken coop, took an egg, and poked the smallest hole in it, and sucked the entire contents out of the shell. Apparently not keen enough to dispose of the evidence, she put the egg back in the hens nest. The next time her mother went out to gather the eggs from the chicken coop, she returned to say, "It's the darnedest thing, this egg is totally empty!"

Having to shell out money for chicken feed, and never getting to eat one of them, my grandmother soon put an end to her husband's chicken farming.

The Victrola

When my mother was a little girl growing up in the 1920's and 30's, there wasn't much to do. There was no T.V., and not everyone had a radio to listen to. In my mother's neighborhood, there was a young woman whose family owned a hand crank Victrola record player. My mother became friends with her, and she would let my mom come over frequently and play her Victrola. My mom had to stand there and wind it up for the record to play. She would do this for a couple of hours at a time, and the young woman didn't seem to mind at all. The records were all in Italian, and a lot of them were operas. This is where my mother's love of music came from, especially classical music. Some of the records were of The Great Enrico Caruso, a famous opera singer from Italy. My mother had been a big fan of his and knew all about him, and how he died from eating too much pasta.

One day the woman invited my mother over to have dinner with her family. The woman's mother came to the table carrying a large platter with a big fish on it. It still had the fins intact, and the eyes were still in it. My mother couldn't eat a bite because the fish seemed to be staring back at her. She never went back to the woman's house to play the Victrola ever again, but the music had already cut lifelong grooves in her soul.

When I was growing up, my mother would let me play her records on her electric phonograph. We would listen to her records for hours. This is where my love of music began; when I began to fall in love with the classics, the operas, the music that had the power to touch and stir my soul. It was grand, and it was beautiful.

My mother owned scores of classical records, which included: Luciano Pavarotti, Mario Lanza, and of course, The Great Enrico Caruso.

The Plague

It was 1929, and it was rare for the average person to own a camera, so if you wanted your picture taken, you had to pay a photographer. This is why there are no pictures of my mom's little sister, Rosie. My mom's family was really poor, and it was difficult to get the money together for things that weren't really necessities, like photographs.

When my mother was about nine years old, she had the responsibility of taking care of her two year old sister when she got home from school. Rosie had dark brown wavy hair, and fair skin. She liked creams, and one time when my mom was supposed to be watching her, Rosie smeared cold cream all over the vanity. One Sunday, Rosie became very ill, and died on Monday morning at dawn. It was May 6, 1929. They said it was Diphtheria.

My mother was huddled on the floor in the corner of the dining room, grieving the loss of her sister. Everyone else was so consumed with their own grief that no one thought to comfort her. Her mother's mother, Grandma Rosa Gagliano, came over and gave Rosie a sponge bath and put a beautiful dress on her to prepare her for the funeral.

My mother's brother, Joe, was tall for his age, and very smart. He loved playing with the other boys and got along very well with them. He would come home and tell my mother stories of going fishing with his friends. She didn't believe him of course, because his friends and he were only about 6 years old at the time. On Saturday morning, Joe became very ill, and so Grandma Rosa came over to help take care of him. He had a high fever and Grandma Rosa took her handkerchief and wiped his face with it. He died later on that same day on May 11, 1929. My mother was still grieving the loss of her sister just days before, so they didn't tell her that Joe had died until the day of his funeral. She was in shock. It was only nine days before his seventh birthday. They said that he died of meningitis.

Grandma Rosa Gagliano was an orphan when Grandpa Gaetano Gagliano met her in a suburb of Baton Rouge, Louisiana. They were married in 1898 in Montagne, Louisiana. She was only 49 years old when she died on May 15, 1929. I'm not sure what they said she died of.

My grandmother, Josephine, must have been so consumed with grief after losing a daughter, a son, and then her mother, all inside of nine days. My mother was to be an only child for a while, because it would be six years before her parents had any more children. Five months later, on October 29 of 1929, the stock market crashed; it was the beginning of the Great Depression.

Grandpa Gagliano died in 1931, almost two years to the day his wife, Rosa, died. My mom said he would take her to the movies when she was a little girl, after grandma had already died. He would have to stop and rest every so often because he had to catch his breath. They said he died of a heart attack.

The Whiskey Barrel

When my father was growing up in Louisiana, his family was really poor. They had a small sugarcane plantation north of New Orleans, and my father and his siblings were expected to help out on the farm. My father never finished school, because his father would come to school and take him home to help chop sugarcane.

When his mom would give birth to a baby, they would fetch Hester, the black midwife down the road. For ten dollars, she would deliver the baby, and then take care of the mother and child for a week. They usually couldn't come up with ten dollars, so they would give her some chickens just for delivering the baby. Trading goods and services was like currency, since real money was sparse. They also tried raising strawberries, but that didn't turn out to be a real money making crop either. My dad said that one time he had a coupon to go to the movies, but that he needed a nickel to go with it, and he couldn't even get the nickel.

My dad finally thought up an easy way to raise some money. His grandfather used to make whiskey, and would keep it in a huge wooden barrel in the barn. My father started sneaking into the barn to steal whiskey out of the barrel so he could sell it. When it became too obvious that there was a large amount of whiskey missing, my father began to add water to the barrel to compensate for the level of whiskey going down. After a while his customers started complaining that the last couple of bottles of whiskey he sold them appeared to be watered down.

With dwindling supply, and ever decreasing quality of product, my father's bootlegging business came to an abrupt end.

My Mother's Wedding

George Schiro and Antoinette Nastasi were married on June 18, 1938, in St. Anthony's Church, in Rockford, Illinois. It was in the Italian part of town, and all the Italians attended mass there.

My mom and dad met while they were both working at the General Electric Radio factory in Rockford, Illinois, in the 1930's. My mother's family, and my father's family, had both relocated to Rockford, Illinois, from Louisiana in hopes of finding work. The city of Rockford, Illinois, had advertised in newspapers in the south for workers to come and relocate there to work in their factories. The ads said that Rockford was the greatest industrial city in America, and that it was the furniture capital of the world. Thousands of workers were needed immediately to fill all the job openings.

My dad was a cabinet maker, and my mom worked in the detailing department making sure everything looked perfect before leaving the factory. All the girls liked my dad and were jealous of my mother because he liked her, and not them. They couldn't figure out what he saw in that skinny girl. One day my mom went to the bathroom, and when she came back, she found that someone had tipped over her can of varnish. The foreman liked my mom and said he would take care of the matter.

My mom soon left the furniture factory and went to Tulsa, Oklahoma for a while to take care of her aunt's children, while her and her husband attended Bible College. My dad wrote my mom a letter asking her to come back to Rockford and marry him. She accepted, and returned to Rockford.

Josephine, my mother's mother, was not happy with the idea of my mom marrying my dad. She didn't like him, because, first of all, he was gae gae, (Pronounced gay gay). It is a Sicilian slang word used to describe people whose ancestors were of Greek origin and had come from the area of Albania or Greece. My father's last name was Schiro (Pronounced ski-row) and his father's ancestors originally came from Albania, and they spoke a different dialect. The Albanians had settled in Sicily, just up the hill from Palermo. Their town was called Piana degli Albanesi. The Albanians, along with hordes of others, exited Sicily in the late 1800's and early 1900's. I'm sure the term my grandmother used was really derogatory, but I haven't been able to find anyone who could tell me the exact meaning of the word. They wanted my mom to marry someone who was 100 % Sicilian, just like them. The reasoning wasn't sound because the Sicilian people are a mixture of many ethnic groups including, the Normans, Romans, Greeks and the Arabs just to mention a few.

The other reason Grandma Josephine didn't like my dad was because he was Catholic, and if my mother married him, she would have to convert to Catholicism. Back in Italy, their family used to be Catholic, but Josephine's father, Gaetano Gagliano, made the decision to leave the Catholic Church after a priest loaned him a bible. Back then, the Pope had issued an edict that people should not own bibles because they were not educated enough to be able to interpret the scriptures properly. But since Gaetano was an altar boy, the priest let him take home a bible to read. He must have been very dedicated, because he studied the bible and came to the conclusion that the Catholics were doing it wrong. When he came to the United States, he apparently found some like-minded Italians and began meeting on Sunday nights in people's homes. The Italian church was born out of these meetings. My mother told me it was really strict, and proceeded to rattle off a long list of don'ts for its members: no drinking, no dancing, no smoking, no shorts, no short dresses, no sleeveless shirts, and the list went on. It sounded like no fun, and it didn't make me want to sign up.

They were downstairs cooking in the summer kitchen one day when my Grandma Josephine was trying to dissuade her from marrying my dad, and things got out of hand. Josephine was so mad at my mom that she was screaming at her, and then she threw a frying pan at her. My mom said she ducked to avoid being hit.

My mom's mind was made up and wedding plans were made despite her mother's protests. When the big day finally arrived, my mother, who was 18 years old at the time, took her girlfriend aside before the ceremony, and asked her where babies came from. No one ever talked about sex back then. I'm not sure if you were supposed to just find out all about it on your wedding night, or what. But this was her entire sex education course, crammed into just a few minutes right before the ceremony. I wonder if this is where the term "blushing bride" comes from.

The wedding was very early in the morning, and after the wedding, everyone went to Josephine's house for breakfast. The wedding went beautifully; however, my mom's parents never came to the wedding because Josephine still did not agree with my mom's choice in a husband. Someone later told my mom that her parents came to the church, but sat outside in their car the whole time, and would not come in.

I really enjoyed growing up Catholic, and all the pleasures it afforded me. I love dancing, and lying on the beach in my swimsuit while drinking a piña colada. And so did my mom.

George & Antoinette

Lights, Camera, Action!

Our father was a camera nut. Most families just have to pose for a family photo at Christmas, or on a birthday, or some impromptu picture. Not our family. There was almost never an impromptu photo. You would think that we were kids of a real movie producer in Hollywood.

Almost everything was scripted and queued. Lights, camera, action! He had a plan, and he would tell us what to do before the camera even started rolling. It was staged and directed. My dad was one of the first people in Rockford, Illinois to own a movie camera. He was a volunteer fireman in the 1950's, but it appears that he spent more time filming the fires than he did fighting them.

It wasn't like it is today where everyone has a camera and video on their phone, or even a small video camera that fits in the palm of your hand. No, it was heavy equipment, tripods, hand crank cameras, video cameras, flood lights, dark rooms, and projectors. Black and white films, silent films, silent films with music dubbed in, and then came the color and sound film. There were portable movie screens, and then there was the big movie screen mounted on the ceiling of our basement, all ready for a night at the theater.

Dad even bought a few movies. We still have copies of the Hawaiian girls dancing the hula, and the movie "Chimp the Fireman". The movies were in black and white, but at least they had sound. My sister and I still cannot forget watching Chimp the Fireman at home on the movie screen. It was the original "flat screen" T.V.

The best production to ever come out of the Schiro Movie Studio was a short film known as "The Tennessee Waltz". It was a black and white film with sound. My sister, Linda, was the star of the production, and my brother, Georgie, was the co-star. It was early 1950's, and my brother was about 11, and my sister was about 10. My sister stood in front and sang along with the song The Tennessee Waltz, and my brother, Georgie, was sitting behind her pretending to drink a bottle of beer while playing with his tie and trying to stick it up over his nose. Between verses in the song, Georgie would get up and dance with her. My sister was such a beautiful young lady and played her part perfectly. My brother, on the other hand was a complete goof off.

When I was growing up we would go downstairs to watch all of dad's home movies. It was usually in the winter, around the Christmas holiday season, when we didn't have anything else to do. Our basement was all fixed up with a kitchen, built in bar, a living room with a fireplace, and even a dance floor. The big movie screen was mounted on the ceiling at the end of the dance floor. My brother would set up the projector and lower the screen. Add a few snacks, and we were ready for movie night.

Some of the films were so old and brittle, that sometimes they would break in the middle of the movie. My brother would have to splice the film together before we could continue. This is why there are "jumps" in the film, because there are more than just a few frames missing. Sometimes the projector would jam and destroy a couple of feet of film at a once. Most of movies were from the 1940's & 1950's which was the height of dad's filmmaking career. Eventually we had all of dad's movies converted to DVD's, and so preserved over 30 years of filmmaking.

I always wanted to be a photographer like my dad, but he never showed me how to develop pictures in a dark room. I guess there is not a lot of point to it nowadays, because everything is now digital. I still like to take pictures, and when I do, everything has to be perfect. I don't like taking pictures with an ugly background, and I don't like it when uninvited tourists stray into my scenery shots. If someone's hair or outfit is messed up, I have to fix it, so it is just right, down to the very last detail.

George the producer, director and camera man,
with his wife Antoinette

My Big Sister

My sister, Linda, was 19 Years old, and had already moved to Chicago to attend college by the time I was born. Despite all odds, my sister grew up to excel at everything she did. Aside from our great aunt Martha who became a nurse in the Navy, I cannot think of any other woman in our family that went to college, and had a career.

Only two generations ago, the women in our family were traditionally illiterate, and were married off even before their sixteenth birthday. My mother had lived through the depression in the 1930's and was so tired of being poor, that she quit high school to take a job at a factory.

Because Linda grew up in our family, by all rights she never should have made it out of a room in the nut house, much less go on to something better and achieve her dreams. Having to navigate the old traditions of our ancestors and the ever present tyranny of our father made life difficult at best.

Our father never told us we could go to college and have a career. He never told us girls that we could be anything in life. As girls, we were expected to just get married and have babies. Being a girl in our family seemed to put us at a great disadvantage from the moment of birth. If we had been boys, our father would have gladly bought us cars, and paid for our tuition to go to the college of our choice.

I was never told I could be anything I wanted. I was always told, "Get a job, work!" That was our ticket to the big time. My mother never even mentioned college to me until I was in my last year of high school. By that time, the notion of college sounded preposterous, before then, it wasn't even a consideration. I think she got the idea from my sister.

My sister had gotten a job at the telephone company in Rockford, Illinois. She saved all her money so she could move to Chicago, and go to secretarial school. No one paid for her tuition or even encouraged her. The odds were against her, but with God's help, she made it anyway.

She graduated from secretarial school, and got a job in downtown Chicago with a big fancy lawyer. And that was only the beginning of her career. She stayed in the Chicago area where she met her husband, Larry. They lived and worked near Chicago, and had two beautiful, intelligent daughters. Their daughters also went to college, and now have careers, because they encouraged them and told them they could.

One day my sister and I were speculating what we could have accomplished in our lives if we had had the emotional and financial support of our families. Despite my parents' lack of support, my sister ended up being an administrative secretary to the assistant superintendent of schools in Naperville, Illinois.

With a little help from the cheerleading section above, she had the courage and perseverance to overcome the obstacles that stood in her way. And I guess that's what life is about; persevering, and never giving up on your dreams.

Me & my big sister Linda

The Baccouso

When I was growing up, my parents used some Italian words in place of some English words, so I did grow up learning some Italian. Mostly though, when they spoke Italian it was so I wouldn't understand what they were talking about. Sometimes my dad would come up to me and begin speaking in his Italian dialect, and then after the first sentence switch to English. For years I had no clue what he was talking about. My dad still had quite an accent, as English was not his first language. His parents, being immigrants, spoke Italian to him, and so my dad never learned English until he attended school. He grew up near New Orleans, and there were a lot of French there. Consequently, my dad learned to speak English with a Cajun accent from the Frenchmen that he went to school with.

One of the Italian words I learned from my parents was "Baccouso". When my dad said that he was going to the bathroom, he said, "I'm going to the Baccouso". So I grew up knowing that this was the Italian word for bathroom. Another word that they used frequently was "CULO", which meant "butt". So when I sat in something and it left a mark, my mother would say, "You got something on your culo". It was a nicer way of saying butt.

When I was about 30 years old I was able to find some Italian classes being held in my city. I would finally be able to study the language of my ancestors, and converse with my parents in Italian. I took four years of Italian language classes. The first three years, I had a teacher named Bruna, who was from Venice. She spoke with a Venetian accent. Then, the next year I had a teacher who was from Rome. She spoke with a Roman accent. The differences in pronunciation and accent left me confused. And after four years of study, my mother said that she could not understand what I was saying when I spoke to her in Italian. My mother began to tell me how to pronounce the words as she knew them. A switch was flipped in my brain. This whole time I had been studying standard Italian from teachers from other parts of Italy that had different pronunciations, and now I realized that my mother spoke only the Sicilian dialect, which is even more of a variation of the language. I was able to pick up on some of the pronunciation differences, so as to compensate for my biased education that I received from my teachers that subjected me to their own dialect.

In any event, all that study of Italian did not go to waste. One year, I went on a missionary trip to Argentina with a pastor and some other missionaries. Four of us stayed with one of the pastor's family that had a good size house. Our hosts only spoke Spanish, but the pastor's mother-in-law (whose house it was), said that her grandparents were Italian, and that they used to speak to her in Italian, so she could understand it pretty well. Also, since Spanish and Italian are real similar, I realized I could get through the trip by speaking the Italian I already knew, coupled with a little help from a small Spanish phrase book

I had picked up. On one of the last days of our trip, we went to the beach in Buenos Aires. I had to squeeze into my swimming suit after being treated to banquets thrown in our honor almost every night for the past week. In every church we visited, the people were so wonderful and gracious. They treated us like kings and queens, and we were served the finest foods every night after the services were over. So there I was on the beach in my swimming suit, it was a one piece, but I was still feeling rather bloated. After some coaxing from Paola, the pastor's wife, I finally decided to get into the water with her. She could tell I was rather apprehensive and asked me why, and I said (using what Spanish I had learned, mixed with the Italian I already knew), "tengo un grande culo". She immediately gasped in shock, and put her hands over her face to hide her horror.

A few years ago I took another Italian class with my friend, Pietro. Our teacher was from Sicily. Her name was Maria and she spoke with a Sicilian accent. At least I could understand the accent really good because my parents had the same accent. In all my years of study of the Italian language there are only two Italian words that my teachers could ever come up with for bathroom. They were; bagno for bathroom, and gabinetto for toilet.

Just a few weeks ago, Ruth Ann, (my mother in law), and I went to the Mascoutah Heritage Museum, which was having a presentation on outhouses. It was extremely interesting. They had a slide show on various outhouses in the area, and they even rated them by functionality and design. They even discussed all the various pet names that people used to refer to this outdoor facility. Of course, among all the names that stood out was "back house". And if you say this with a really thick Sicilian accent, it sounds like this: BACCOUSO.

I am again perusing my Italian language education. This year my teacher is an American. Her name is Barbara, and she has an American accent.

Incidentally, I'm not sure that using the word "CULO" as a replacement for the word "butt" is a good idea.

Ketchup,
The American Sugo

Sugo, [su · go] noun, a sauce made with tomatoes.

(Pronounced; Soogoo)

Many years ago, the Italian peasants used to cook all of their vegetables and meats in a seasoned tomato sauce, because tomatoes were very plentiful. Italians call this sugo, (Americans simply refer to this as spaghetti sauce.) They would even put some hard boiled eggs in it. When they took the meat and vegetables out, they were covered with sugo.

My father was the first generation born in America, and he grew up near New Orleans, Louisiana, on a small plantation. Living on a farm, his family continued cooking just like they did in the old country. They had plenty of produce, and simmered everything in a pot of sugo. Consequently, my father was accustomed to having almost every meal covered with tomato sauce. Over the years society became more industrialized, there were better economic conditions, and cooking habits changed considerably. They moved up north and no longer lived on a plantation, where they grew all their own produce. No longer did they cook everything in a pot of sugo.

Dad loved his sugo. He missed having sugo with all his meals. So when ketchup was invented, it must have been one of the best days of his life. Ketchup was the American Sugo. It was instant sugo in a bottle, no more simmering tomatoes in a pot all day long. You could put it on anything, anytime; it was always there in the fridge waiting for you. And he did put it on practically everything: scrambled eggs, fried bologna, fried potatoes, Italian sausage, hot dogs, and hamburgers to name just a few, and of course, steak. Oh, and let's not forget the raw oysters, but that's another story.

Nuns Are People Too

In the first and second grades, I attended St. Edwards Catholic School. I had to wear a uniform that consisted of a blue and white plaid jumper and a white button up blouse. In the years that followed, I developed an emotional allergy to the wool blended plaid. The school was run entirely by an order of nuns that was very strict.

These nuns wore a habit that covered them from head to toe. The only thing you could see was part of their face sticking out of their "headgear", and occasionally, their hands would come out from under the front of their habit to hit you with a ruler or write on the chalkboard. They had no hair, or ears, or even a neck, and I never even saw if they had feet. Coupled with the phlegmatic personalities, there was nothing there that indicated to me that there were humans hiding under the riggings, and I always thought they were part of the divine hierarchy that went like this: God the Father, God the Son, God the Holy Spirit, Angels, and lastly Nuns, who were sent down here to earth to take care of us children. Reverend Mother was the principal, and she had a wooden paddle with holes drilled in it to enforce the school's commandments. I know this because I got a glimpse of it in her office as she was swinging it towards my behind.

Sister Charles Catherine was my second grade teacher. During school hours, Sister would take us downstairs to the bathrooms. She took us girls into the bathroom, which had no doors on the stalls, so there was no such thing as privacy. Sister would stand in front of the stalls, like a Gestapo guard, with her arms and hands folded under part of her habit, and police all the movements in the bathroom. Freud would have reasoned that this is where performance anxiety issues stem from. And as far as the boys' bathroom, I have no idea what went on in there, but I would guess that there are a lot of Catholic men from my class right now with ED issues.

Before third grade, our family had moved to the end of the city limits, which put us in a different parish. There was a church and school only about three blocks away from our new house. It was St. Rita's, where we were going to attend mass, and I would attend the school. It was such a modern church that they even said mass in English instead of Latin.

My mom took me to the new school to register me for the third grade. I would have to wear a uniform that consisted of a blue and white plaid jumper, and a white button up blouse. We went into the office, and there was a nice lady at the desk that helped my mom fill out all the forms. She was wearing a white short sleeve blouse, a brown skirt that was just below her knees, and tennis shoes. She also had a brown and white scarf on her head to keep her hair in place. I also noticed that she had arms and legs, and even a neck. I heard my mother address her as "Sister".

The Black Box

Growing up Catholic in the 1960's and "70's, was such an…experience. Yes, that's what it was, an experience. I guess I almost enjoyed mass for the most part, but going to confession was one part of being catholic that I could do without.

When you are in second grade you have to go through catechism, which is learning all the teachings of the church, and also memorizing prayers such as the one you have to recite from memory when you go to confession. After you complete catechism class, you are ready to make your first confession. Then, after you make your first confession comes the big day when you will take your first communion. I don't remember my first confession. I must have blacked out, and came to just in time to don my fancy white first communion dress. The really good part of your first communion is that it is customary for people to give you cards and or gifts, slash money, if you are lucky.

Through the years I was made to go to confession regularly, because I went to a catholic school. When you attend a catholic school, you also attend mass regularly each week with the whole school, and to insure your soul from hellfire, it was mandatory to go to confession before receiving communion during mass. When it was time to go to confession, everyone dreaded the confessional, which I unaffectionately named "The Black Box". It was really scary to open the door to this room that was smaller than a broom closet, but larger than a breadbox. There was only enough room to walk in and kneel down, there was no space between the kneeler and the wall, only enough space to stand up and exit the room. Once a person entered and shut the door, there was only a very dim light that would enable you to find the door handle and make an escape. When you knelt down, in front of you was this screen, and behind it, it was possible to make out the outline of a figure with a hood over his head, facing a different direction, all to insure your anonymity. How they figured a small child would feel secure enough not to crap their pants in this situation was beyond me.

When I was about 12, my father made to go to confession. When I entered the black box, I said the words that the nuns had made me memorize when I went through catechism at about 8 years of age; "Oh my God, *I am hardly sorry,* for having offended thee".

I continued with my confession, and then proceeded to "invent" some sins to tell to the priest, since I was innocent and only there under duress from my father anyway. On my next visit at least I would have some legitimate sins to confess.

I was only in the second grade when I had to memorize the prayer we were supposed to say in the confessional. Apparently I was too young to even understand what the words meant. It wasn't until I was in my thirties that I found out that I had been saying the wrong words all along, and realized that I was really supposed to be saying; "Oh my God, *I am heartily sorry, for having offended thee*".

Picking Worms

My whole family loved to fish. It was a cheap hobby, and all you needed was worms or minnows. My dad and brother always caught a lot of fish, and I didn't do too bad myself. My mother also fished, or at least she had a fishing license. Mostly she would sit in the cockpit of our boat and drink Mai ties while my dad kept an eye on her poles. That was really nice of him, because he already had two poles of his own in the water, but he didn't seem to mind.

Coming from meager beginnings, my parents would always do whatever they could to save money. One of the things that my dad saved money on was the dew worms that they used as bait for fishing. They never bought worms, they were free. We always went and picked our own. When I was about ten years old, my dad and brother would let me go with them to pick worms. The worms grew in the grass at the golf course, and they sprung up after the sun went down, because the dew watered the grass, and it caused the worms to grow out of the ground.

We would wait until it was really dark outside, then we would drive to the golf course on Sandy Hollow Road, after it was closed for the day. We would take our flashlights, and shine the light on the ground, and if we saw a worm, we had to grab hold of it quickly, and pull. They were really slimy and slippery and hard to hold onto, and if we didn't pick them really fast, the earth's gravity would cause them to be sucked into the center of the earth, and we would never see them again.

We would take them home and put them in this wooden box that my brother had made, which was full of Buss Bedding. Buss Bedding is made of an unknown substance that looks like wet newspaper mash. It is supposed to keep the worms tasting good, and preserve their flavor, however, I have never conducted a taste test to prove if this is really true.

If we got a whole bunch, my dad would put them in small Styrofoam containers, and sell them at his hardware store for under a dollar a dozen. It seemed like a lot of work for so little money. After my dad sold his store, he didn't have anywhere to sell his worms. But, I guess he got enough money from the sale that he was now rich enough to pay someone else to pick his worms.

The Kiss

If you have ever seen the movie, The Godfather, you would understand the meaning behind all those kisses exchanged, not just between members of the family, but between friends, business associates, and even enemies.

In some cultures, a kiss is not just a token of affection. Sometimes, there is no affection involved at all, most of the time it was all about respect. It was about loyalty, and sometimes, it was about an agreement. Or maybe it was about betrayal, or even the kiss of death.

When my parents would have relatives over, never mind if I had never even met them before, I would be expected to kiss them. There was no getting out of it. It would have even reflected badly on my parents for me to refuse or to even have had to be persuaded. I knew I would have to kiss almost everyone that entered my house, whether I wanted to or not, whether I even liked them or not.

I remember as a young girl, when it was time for bed, I had to kiss my father goodnight. He would sit in his recliner like it was a throne, assume a kingly posture, and turn his cheek for me to kiss, and if he was in an affectionate mood, he would offer me the other cheek to kiss also. If he was angry with me, he never offered me the other cheek to kiss. My father never kissed me back.

I only remember my father kissing my brother one time, and it was after he had been seriously injured and was in the hospital. He was concerned for his life. It was the one and only time I remember my dad kissing my brother, but I noticed my brother usually kissed my dad.

You didn't have to love the person you were kissing, but to withhold a kiss was tantamount to a slap in the face. It was an insult. I wouldn't doubt that there were wars started over this in the old country. Even today, there are those that have to show loyalty and respect to others through a token of a kiss; like having to kiss the pope's ring.

Kissing my mother and my sister was quite different. We used to kiss each other on the cheek, but as we got older, it seems we really didn't want to have lipstick on our cheeks messing up our makeup, so we just always kissed on the lips. Now that's how you know someone really has affection for you, if they kiss you on the lips. It's not a mushy type of kiss, just a peck. But it just feels too informal for me to kiss my sister on the cheek. In the American culture this is definitely not the norm, and very rarely do I attempt to kiss my American friends, because I know they are not used to this custom, and they might feel very uncomfortable. My friend, Victoria, is one of the few friends that I have that feels comfortable kissing me, but then again she is half Italian and we've know each other for over 35 years.

By the time my father was about 89 years old, he had developed dementia. He had actually become a nicer person since the onset of the disease. I had gone over to their house for a visit, and after I had been there for a while, my father was walking past where I was sitting and said, "Did I give you a hug and kiss yet?" I was so shocked I almost went into a coma. I could not ever remember my father giving *me* a kiss. It took developing dementia for him to forget about me giving him the traditional kiss of respect, and for him to offer me a kiss of affection.

The Mammoni

My brother, Georgie, lived at home till he got married at the ripe old age of 40. He was what the Italians call a Mammoni, a single man who lives at home with mama and papa, and sees no need to move out on their own. And really, there wasn't any need for it. Italian families are close knit, and are used to having more than one generation living together. It is customary for the children to live at home until they marry, and sometimes even after. Even today it is part of the family culture in Italy, where over 50 percent of single men and 40 percent of single women live at home with mama and papa. Only in America do we try to shove our offspring out of the nest with the force of a catapult soon after high school graduation. If you want to see real live failure to launch, just go visit the average Italian family in Italy.

Being a Mammoni came with many benefits: mama did his laundry, she bought the groceries, cooked all the meals, and washed all the dishes. He didn't have to pay rent or utilities or even clean his room. (He wasn't messy, but he never dusted or vacuumed his own room, I actually did!)

At Christmas my parents asked him what he wanted, and he usually said clothes, because he never went shopping for himself, except for maybe shoes, but then again I never knew him to go into a store that sold anything other than ammo or minnows.

Since my brother was 20 years old when I was born, it was like I grew up with two fathers instead of a father and a brother. He would boss me around and I would yell at him, "You're not my dad, you can't tell me what to do!" When I was a baby and mom and dad went out, he said I started screaming the minute mother left the house, and didn't stop until she returned, because I was a mama's baby. When I was older he had to babysit me every Saturday night when mom and dad went out. He would take me to our Cousin Ginger's house, who was also my fairy godmother, along with her husband, Bill who was my fairy godfather. I would watch Heehaw on T. V. while they all played cards in the kitchen.

My brother loved hunting, and when he got stuck with me, he would take me pheasant hunting with him. To really pheasant hunt correctly, you need a hunting dog to track down the birds. He didn't have a dog, so I had to play the part of the hunting dog. I had to walk through the fields 50 paces in front of him in order to flush out the pheasants. I was supposed to sniff them out and chase them so they would take flight, because it was only legal to shoot them when they were in the air. I was not a good hunting dog apparently, because we never got any pheasants.

My brother also worked with my father and mother at the family business, which was an Ace Hardware store. My mom did all the bookkeeping and was a cashier. My dad waited on a lot of customers, mixed paint; make keys, cut pipe, and repaired windows and screens. My brother put together all the orders and checked them in along with a whole lot of other stuff. I even worked there in the summers, and sometimes after school, and when I turned twelve, I got to be a cashier.

When my dad was in his early sixties, he decided he wanted to retire. He had always assumed that my brother would take over the family business, but my brother didn't want to run the business without the help of my parents. So my dad decided to sell the store. Thus began my brother's retirement at the age of 34. I was 14 at the time, and I was stuck living in a retirement home.

My dad always had a boat on the Mississippi River, and when my family retired, we practically lived on the boat in the summer. My dad loved boats, but could never afford them, so he built them himself, being an expert carpenter.   The last boat he had built was a 35 foot long cabin cruiser. When my dad sold his store, he had enough money to sell the boat he had built and buy his dream boat. It was a 46 foot long Chris Craft Roamer. It had two heads, and two staterooms; my parents got the captain's quarters in the aft cabin, my brother always slept on the pull out bed in the salon, and I got the forward V berth all to myself. Georgie and I lived on the boat all summer. We would go home once a week to help dad mow the lawn, and for mom to do our laundry and get us more food. Then we would drive back down to the boat, and mom and dad would come down later for a long weekend, but head back on Monday or Tuesday. I could never figure out why they wanted to go home, or what they could find to do there on land. Georgie and I would fish and swim all day. We did this all summer, until I had to go back to school in the fall. At the end of the boating season it was too cold to go to the boat on the weekends, and so came the time to take it out of the water and put it on dry dock. Such was our lives for the next few years.

Five years after he retired, Georgie met Cindy, the love of his life, while boating on the Mississippi River. They got married when he was 40 years old, thus ending his retirement, and his life as a Mammoni, as now he was to take on the responsibility of a family.

Georgie

The Entertainer

My parents were really social people and loved throwing parties. When they built their dream house, it was practically designed for entertaining.

My parents had gone to the big Ace Hardware warehouse in Chicago, Illinois, and picked out all these fancy light fixtures for the house before they built it, and then decorated the rooms around the light fixtures. For the formal dining room, my mother picked out this big gilded chandelier from Spain that had oodles of crystals hanging from it. It was suspended precisely over the exact center of the dining room table.

The formal living room was decorated in Italian provincial, because, they were Italian. With the exception of possibly one end table, every table top was made of white marble, and supported by some Italian column or cherub, painted white and accented with gold gilding. There was this humongous glass lamp in the corner that was shaped like a, well I don't know exactly. It was fat in the middle and tapered on both ends, whatever shape that is. It was suspended by a chain on a hook, and then the chain was draped to another hook before trailing down to the floor, where it was plugged into the outlet. The shag carpet was a popular color green that I hated, but was in everyone's house in the late 60's and early 70's. My mother had special curtains made from a white jacquard fabric.

They had swag valances, but instead of shears, there were venetian blinds. I only remember opening the venetian blinds a few times. It was my job to do it because I was strong, and the blinds were so heavy due to the window's great expanse. Also, someone had to try and lift them as the other person pulled the cord. After about 25 years or so the individual cords in the blinds broke, causing the blinds to sag. They were eventually replaced with plain shears, probably from JC Penny's.

My father had finished the basement with the intent of entertaining a lot of people, and having all the relatives over for the holidays. There was a complete kitchen down stairs, and a banquet hall with those long banquet tables. He had a built in bar, a family room with a brick fireplace, and even a dance floor with speakers in the ceiling to pipe in the dance music. He even bought a pool table, and set it up in the back room before putting up the stair railing. I know this because my Uncle Bill wanted to buy the pool table when my mom sold her house, but we couldn't figure out how to get it up the stairs, even after it was taken apart. My dad hadn't forgotten even one detail, as he even put in a coat rack and a bathroom.

Under the stairs leading down to the basement, my father built a closet. My mom put my toy box in it, so I always had somewhere to keep my toys out of sight. When my mom sold her house to move into a retirement home, I helped her get rid of a lot of furnishings. I moved my old toy box out of that closet, only to discover that there was a floor safe located directly underneath it. It was unlocked, and to my dismay, empty; no family jewels, no treasure of any kind.

The basement was used especially during the holidays. First came Christmas Eve. The Sicilians were big on celebrating Christmas on Christmas Eve. That's when we opened our presents from each other. My mother fixed mountains of food. She had food cooking in the two ovens that were in the upstairs kitchen, and she had food cooking in oven in the downstairs kitchen. Not to mention the stovetops in both kitchens. My mother would set up a buffet on the banquet table that was against the wall. The main food of Christmas Eve was always stuffed artichokes and shrimp. It was a Sicilian tradition. To this day, I still make artichokes and shrimp for Christmas. Of course she also made a ham, sweet potato casserole, green bean casserole, pies, cuccidati (italian fig cookies), and other italian cookies. I couldn't list everything she made here, it would take too long. After we all pigged out, we would sit around the fireplace and open our presents to each other. Then, I don't know how we even managed it, but we would go to midnight mass.

Then came Christmas morning, and we would get up and repeat the whole thing over again, except for mass. Christmas day was when we got to open our gifts from Santa. Then my mom would cook more food, but since it was Christmas day, we would also have pasta, along with more of the same things we had the previous night. This is the day when all the other relatives would come over, because they had already celebrated Christmas with their families the night before. They also brought more food with them when they came.

Then there were the New Year's Eve parties for their friends. Most of them seemed to be people that lived in the neighborhood, or that went to our church. Some of the guests lived so close, they just walked over. I, of course, would be upstairs watching TV and letting in the guests, and directing them to the basement. I was just a kid, so I was not invited to the party.

Since my parents had the best "party house", whenever there was some kind of family reunion, it was always held at my parent's house. If it was summer, we could play games outside in the big yard. I remember setting up the croquet set all over the yard, and leaving it there till it was time to mow the lawn. Then we had a bocce ball set, and Jarts. I loved playing Jarts, but I'm sure they don't make them anymore because they are dangerous and could probably be used as a weapon. But my family never killed anyone with a "Jart", so I considered them fairly safe. However, I'm sure my great grandmother Antonia could have used it for a weapon. They were huge darts about a foot long with a big metal point on the end that you had to throw into this circle which was just a big plastic hoop.

My mother loved to cook, and was always inviting people over for dinner. She loved throwing formal dinner parties in the dining room. She would always invite the parish priests and nuns at St. Rita's over for dinner. I attended the school there at St. Rita's parish, and my mother was always inviting the whole faculty over for dinner. I could barely make it through the evening, and I didn't even have to eat with them. I ate alone at the kitchen table, and hid in the living room as quietly as I could. I just couldn't believe I had to put up with my teachers at home as well as school; I was excruciatingly uncomfortable the whole night, and I couldn't wait for them to leave.

I miss my parents' parties, even if I didn't get invited to some of them as a kid. I miss socializing with people and having a good time. Someday, I'm going to build my dream house with entertaining in mind and throw big parties. It's going to have a built in bar, and a dance floor, but instead of piped in music, maybe I'll have a live band.

The Angel

When I was pregnant with my son, I would think how much I wanted a boy, but I really felt like I was carrying a girl. I kept telling God how much I wanted a boy. I had one ultrasound at my doctor's office, when I was about three months pregnant, and they said everything was fine so I didn't need to have any more ultrasounds. Back in those days they didn't do ultrasounds on pregnant women unless there was a problem. People would bring me baby clothes, and I would jokingly hold them up to my stomach to "see if they fit". Throughout my pregnancy I continued to tell God how much I wanted a boy.

One morning, when I was about six and a half months pregnant, when the sun was just starting to come up, I had a....dream? It was so real it was more like a vision. On the side of the bed where I was sleeping, an angel appeared. She was beautiful. She was wearing a white gown and was surrounded by light. I remember her having big beautiful wings and light golden brown hair. In front of her was a little girl. This little girl looked like a miniature me, Italian, with black hair. I don't remember what she was wearing. I was so frightened in the dream that I tried to scream or move, but I was paralyzed. The angel was leaving and taking my little girl and I couldn't do anything to stop her. The angel was disappearing as I began to wake up, but I was still paralyzed and trying to scream.

When I awoke, the angel was gone, but I was still trying to scream. When I had fully come to my senses and realized the angel was gone, I stopped trying to scream, and the paralysis had left my body. From that moment on, I knew I was having a boy.

When I was about nine and a half months pregnant, my doctor decided that he needed to induce labor, so I went home and packed a bag and left for the hospital. On February 17, 1982 I gave birth to my beautiful 7lb., 11oz. baby boy, Anthony Collin. He was just what I had ordered!

Me and my son Anthony

Dogs

When I was married to my ex, he loved dogs. Big dogs. I preferred small dogs, or a cat. One time we had three Dobermans at once. They were the biggest babies ever. They didn't even know they were dogs, they thought they were people, and we treated them accordingly.

One morning I woke up thinking my husband was hogging all the covers. I gave the covers a hefty tug to recover my portion, but they didn't budge. I rolled over to find one of the dogs lying on top of the covers in the middle of the bed.

My husband worked nearby, so he would come home for lunch every day. I would make his lunch and put it on a plate so it would be waiting for him when he came home. One particular day I was in the living room when he came home. He went into the kitchen and sat down at the table, and asked where his lunch was. I hollered to him that it was on the plate, as I wondered what was wrong with his eyes. I went into the kitchen to investigate, only to find an empty plate without as much as a crumb on it.

One evening I was cooking Hamburger Helper in a cast iron skillet on our gas stove. I went to the bathroom, and by the time I came out, the youngest Doberman was just finishing up licking any remaining molecules that were left of the Hamburger Helper, which was still simmering on top of the lit gas range.

Finally, I came home from work one evening to find my male Doberman, Jimbo, lying on my son's bed in a huge pile of what looked like fluffy white clouds of cotton, and shredded rags, all arranged in a huge circle around him. I identified it as my son's bedding, from as recent as that morning before I had left for work. It was now a huge nest that would have been more befitting a pterodactyl.

I now have two large house plants in the dining room; they are getting so big I can barely squeeze by them to sit in my chair. My doctor says that if the stress of taking care of the plants doesn't raise my blood pressure, it might be ok to get a goldfish.

The Dig

For the first time in many years, I was getting a tax refund instead of having to pay. I was so excited. I was going to put it in the bank and build my nest egg. But the more I thought about it, the more I wanted to do something special with it. I decided that I wanted to go on a trip.

I asked my 13 year old son if he wanted to go to Mexico with me. I pleaded and I begged, I might have even graveled, but he wouldn't give his consent to go to Mexico with his mother.

At the time, I had a subscription to a magazine called Biblical Archeology Review. I had always found archeology to be a very interesting subject, and when I was in college, I even considered taking it as a major. One day, I was looking through the magazine and noticed all these ads for places that you could volunteer to work on an archeological dig, right next to the big wigs.

After looking through the ads in the magazine, I had made up my mind that I was going to volunteer to work on an archeological expedition in Israel. The very next day I started making phone calls to inquire about them. The first call I made was to a very groggy and upset man with a thick accent. He was ranting about how I woke him up in the middle of the night. I hadn't even thought about it, the advertisement just gave a number, not the address, so I didn't exactly know where I was calling. Apparently we were in totally opposite time zones. The next phone call was more carefully placed to an establishment in California, The Israel Archaeological Society. I spoke to the nice man, at the other end of the phone, and told him I would like to come out for a week. He said I needed to be there longer than a week, because that was only long enough to get over the jet lag. I told him that because I owned my own business, I didn't want to miss a lot of work. By the time I hung up from talking with him, he had convinced me into committing almost a month in the Middle East. I would be joining an archeological dig that was already in progress.

I packed a backpack (this mode of travel was recommended by the travel guide), and a map of Israel, and flew off. My mother was frantic. She said I needed to go on some organized tour, with people I knew, and real luggage, not just fly off by myself with a backpack. "I'm meeting people there", I said.

I flew into Tel Aviv and took a shuttle from the airport, and into town, where they dropped me at the bus station. I took my backpack, and got out my map and tried to decipher the street names in the map, and match them up against the street signs which had different spellings of the same words. I learned that "Shlomo" is the same as "Solomon". It took me two hours of wandering around Tel Aviv at night, in the dark, to learn this, while carrying my backpack on my back.

I finally arrived at the hostel I was to stay at. It was so late at night, that the lady of the hostel was upset because I wanted to take a shower, and she had to go to the fourth floor to get me a towel. She thought that if she complained long and loud enough about having to go upstairs to get a towel that I would change my mind about taking a shower. However, it had been two days since I showered, due to having a long layover at the Paris airport. I felt sorrier for me than I did for her, and she finally relented and went to get me that towel. I had just finished my shower when one of my roommates came in and introduced herself as Debra. She was from California. She was also as crazy as I was to fly off by herself to join the dig, but she said her husband would be joining her later. After my shower, I was shown to my room, which I was to share with nine other women.

The next day for breakfast we had the standard Middle Eastern fare: pita bread, goat cheese, sardines, cucumbers and tomatoes. I had never had sardines for breakfast before. Karen, a very rugged looking, young junior high school teacher showed me the ropes. She was dressed more like a mercenary, and her luggage looked like a military issue duffle bag. She was detained at every border crossing. After we had finished eating breakfast, she started wrapping up any remaining scraps of food in whatever she could find, and stashing it in her shoulder bag. She explained to me that I might want to "take something for later, just in case". So I did likewise. Then the fearless leader of our group, instructed us to keep our hats on at all times, or wear a turban to protect our head from the hot desert sun. Also, he warned us to never go anywhere without a bottle of water. I took all of these lessons to heart. Never did I leave a meal table without a "doggy bag" and a full bottle of water.

After a couple days of traveling around the Sea of Galilee, we finally arrived in Jerusalem where we were going to join the dig. We were staying at Christ Church Guest House in the old city of Jerusalem. I was assigned my room in which I had five roommates. That's six women, and one bathroom. Not to mention very little water pressure. Also the temperature of the water depended on the temperature of the holding tank on the roof of the building. The hot and cold temperature handles were there just for decoration only.

The archeological dig was located in the old Jerusalem. It was just to the right of the Wailing Wall, under what is called Robinson's Arch, which was one of the staircases that led from the old temple to the street below it. Some of us chopped away mounds of rubble left over from bombings using a pickaxe; others carefully brushed away dirt and sand with a paint brush, all in hopes of finding the greatest archeological discovery of the century. The only objects of notoriety found on the dig while I was there were the jawbone of an ass, and a handle to what could have been a brush of some sort. Not to mention, literally hundreds, if not thousands of pieces of mosaic rock that were once arranged to form great works of art.

At lunch time they brought us each a bottle of almost cold water, which tasted like soap, and a bagela, which was a small loaf of bread which tasted like a bagel. Here is where it was advantageous to have stolen any remaining food scraps from earlier meals, as just plain bread and water for a meal was less than I was accustomed to having. Someone must have complained because a few days later, the lunch menu got an upgrade to a can of almost cold pop that tasted like soap, a bagela, and an apple.

There were no bathrooms located on the dig site, so every time I had to go to the bathroom, I had to go through a security checkpoint, walk across the compound opposite the Wailing Wall, and then over to the bathrooms. It was July. In the desert. I was wearing a sleeveless shirt and shorts. Not even really short shorts. But as soon as I got near the Wailing Wall, women would come running toward me to cover my naked parts up with what looked like Israeli flags. They put one around my shoulders, and one around my waist like a skirt so as to hang down and cover my knees. Apparently God lives in the remaining stones of the Wailing Wall and he doesn't want to see my shoulders or knees.

After we had put in our time on the dig, it was time to do a little sightseeing before flying off home. We left for Jordan to see the "Treasury" in Petra, and then we traveled through the Sinai desert on our way to Mt. Sinai. We stopped somewhere in the middle of the desert for lunch. I ordered one of the four available menu items which was a piece of pita bread with some goat cheese and a slice of tomato all roasted over a flame. It was a slight upgrade from the now stale food I had stashed in my shoulder bag.

After we had visited St. Catherine's monastery, which was located at the base of Mt Sinai, we checked into an "inn". That is the nicest name I could think of to call it, which was located precisely in the middle of nowhere. This is where Moses and the Israelites got lost for forty years in the desert because there isn't anything there to tell you that you had been going in circles. One night we were sitting around the dinner table at the inn when they came around to serve our meal. One man came around putting meat on our plates. My roommate was sitting next to me, and she asked the man what kind of meat it was, and he replied "good meat". She grumbled back, "Well I'm not eating that". To which the man on my left and I simultaneously said, "I'll eat it!" I looked at the man and said, "I'll split it with you". When she realized that we were arguing about who was going to eat her dinner, she shut up about the Unidentified Food Object, and ate without further complaining. We were in the middle of the desert, and unless you stashed some rations from some other meal, and or country, you weren't getting anything until the next day.

My journey ended in Egypt where I boarded a French plane for the flight home. The stewardess said I needed to put my shoulder bag under my seat, but the guy in back of me was so tall, his feet were sticking out under my seat and I couldn't put my pack there. I could barely put my own feet down in front of my seat. It was going to be a long flight home. When the stewardess tried to grab my bag to put it in an overhead, I clutched it tight to my chest and yelled at her, "You can't take this, my food and my water's in here". Everyone around me stared at me like I was a nut case. I had to explain I just spent a month in the desert on an archeological dig where at times we had meager food rations, and how they told us not to go anywhere without our water.

Maybe the French stewardesses misunderstood and thought I was an archeologist, because from that point on the stewardesses gave me first class treatment. They secretly called me into the galley to give me the leftover delicacies from first class, like strawberries dipped in chocolate and champagne. It was going to be a good flight home.

Annette on her journey to the top of Mount Sinai

The Designated Driver

When my mom was in her late 70's, she didn't like to drive a lot, and my dad had already quit driving. That's why she always called me up and asked me to drive her places. I would come over, and we would get into her car, because she had a big Lincoln continental.

One day, my mom called me up to ask me to be a designated driver for her and a friend. She said that a friend's husband died, and that she wanted me to pick her and her girlfriend up, and take them to the funeral. I thought, well my mom is almost 80; I can understand why she doesn't want to drive. The woman whose husband had died was well beyond 80, and so was her deceased husband.

I thought it was odd that the funeral was being held at Giovanni's restaurant and convention center. Occasionally, I would join my friend, Bonnie, there for a chocolate martini at Big Al's bar, which was part of the restaurant. As we entered the large hall I noticed that it looked more like a wedding reception. There were big round banquet tables, dressed in white linen table cloths and white napkins. There was a buffet, and an open bar. I didn't think we were late, but as we came in I noticed a bunch of guys sitting around one of the tables, and they were already pretty drunk. I thought it was odd because I thought I was supposed to be at a funeral. That's what my mom said anyway.

We were sitting at a table with the grieving widow and Monsignor Wahl. Monsignor comes from the same Wahl family that owned the Wahl razor and shaver company. He liked to travel the world and would take large groups of people with him. My mom traveled with him around the world, and even went to China with him.

The ceremony began, and Monsignor Wahl got up and proceeded to do a roast of the deceased. He talked about how they were neighbors, and how he would go next door and talk to him, and try to convince him to become a Christian. Apparently, the deceased was an atheist, and his wife was a devout catholic that attended St. Rita's Catholic Church in Cherry Valley, Illinois, where Monsignor Wahl was the pastor.

Monsignor Wahl said he could never convince the man to come to church. He didn't want to hear anything Monsignor had to say, but now that he was dead, Monsignor said that he was going to get the last word in and preach at his funeral, and the deceased could have nothing to say about it.

About the time Monsignor got up to speak, I finally realized I was at an Irish funeral. The only difference between an Irish wedding and an Irish funeral is, of course, one less drunk.

Time for Tea

It was the end of May and they had already shut off the heat. I was freezing. I'm Sicilian, and my thin Mediterranean blood couldn't take it. It was cold and damp, and worse when I went outside. The big stone building that used to be a convent was over 450 years old, and was now a boarding school for a ministry in the south of England. It was in the middle of nowhere, and once you were there, you were stranded and off the grid. This was also at a time before everyone had cell phones, and Wi-Fi was almost unheard of. I was lucky to get a taxi to come out there and get me when it was time to leave.

I was attending a ministry training class that was to be 21 days long, from nine in the morning till nine at night. I was dreading the grueling schedule, and not sure how I was going to make it through the long days.

The first day of class we started at 9 o'clock, and then, at 10:30 sharp, in mid sentence, the instructor looked at his watch and said, "Oh my, it's time for tea". We then all adjourned into one of the ground floor rooms that looked like a pub, where we were served our choice of hot beverages, mainly tea, with cookies of course. By the time we were back in the classroom, there was only one hour remaining until lunch, which was served promptly at noon. All the meals were severed boarding house style, and all the students ate together at every meal. We would sit at these long tables, and servers would come around and put our rations on our plate. After lunch, we went into the pub, and again we served hot beverages of our choice, mainly tea. And now we had some free time until the next session. Most of us chose to take a nap. The next session didn't last long because we had to go to dinner, and then we were served hot beverages of our choice, mainly tea. Then the last session was grueling because it was two long hours with no tea. After the last session was over, we went downstairs for supper drinks where we were served hot beverages of our choice, even tea, with cookies. Then, some of us piled like sardines into someone's car, and went into town to get fish and chips at this little stand to compensate for starving at dinner. Such was our daily routine for the next 20 days.

The school mainly served food that they grew themselves in their greenhouse or livestock that was raised on the property. This accounted for the food rationing, and the fact that meat was rarely placed on our plates. I could also tell that the cauliflower crop had done well this year.

The school raised sheep in the pasture across from the building. On our breaks we would stroll around the property to get some exercise, and sometimes watch the sheep in the pasture for excitement. One day, one of the other students said that we were going to have meat at dinner (it was Sunday), I asked how he knew this, and he answered back, "I counted the sheep, and there is one missing." Sure enough, at dinner time, we had meat on our plate. A lot of students weren't used to eating lamb and didn't care for it. I was kind enough to let them put it on my plate to get rid of it.

The students came from all over the world; there were 35 of us in all. Since we were all living together in this old convent, we had to learn to do things together and share everything. We all had to share the one payphone downstairs, the one T.V. located in the big living room downstairs, and the only computer in the whole building. I went downstairs one afternoon during one of the breaks and found about 25 or more of the students huddled around the one small television in the living room. They said they were watching football and asked if I wanted to join them. I found out it was really soccer, the English version of football. One day, for excitement, a man took it upon himself to organize a group to solve a crossword puzzle he found in the Sunday paper.

For some reason I had the impression that being in England was not going to be much different than being in the U.S... I found out that even though they speak the English language, there were a lot of differences in use of vocabulary words and colloquialisms. I also found that there were a lot of cultural differences that I didn't expect.

I had been trying to wash my clothes at night after the staff had finished doing the school laundry in the limited facilities, but it was difficult to share the washers and dryers with the staff and 35 students. I wanted to wear clean clothes every day and smell nice. I even tried to take a shower every day despite the lack of water pressure, and hot water, if I had failed to get up early enough. It was all brought to naught one day when an English lady came up to me, and in a heated tone of voice, hurled an accusation toward me "You Americans! You change your clothes every day, don't you?" I was speechless; I didn't know what to say.

Over the next week I took note of what my classmates were wearing, and I actually observed a woman who wore the same outfit every day for a week. I was one of very few people that had a totally different outfit on every day. Based on my observations, I really was guilty of changing my clothes everyday as charged.

The Pope Isn't Coming to Dinner

I bought this really nice china to replace the old pattern that I had fallen out of love with. It had been almost twenty years and my tastes had changed. It was never a complete set anyway, and if I was to complete the set now, it would cost me more than to just buy a whole new set.

The new set was so beautiful. It was Prince Albert Royal Doulton, with the Country Roses pattern on it. And it was made in England, not China. I might have used it once a year, if it was very special occasion, and if I invited someone special over. But I didn't even use it for Christmas or Easter. I always went to my mom's, and we used her china. Then when my sister took over having the holidays at her house, we used her china.

Mine was so beautiful sitting the in the china cabinet where I could look at it as I passed by. I was waiting for some special day to use my china. One day I had the realization that the Pope was not coming to dinner or even tea. There might never be a momentous occasion to use my china. I may never be visited by a real important person like the president, or the Pope. I could wait till I die, and my china might never come out of the closet.

I decided to start using my old china that I no longer liked as much for everyday dishes. One of my friends came over for pizza and I served it on my old china. They remarked how special they felt. I didn't say anything, but I was thinking if they only knew that these were now the new paper plates. I started looking for excuses to pull out the good stuff. I held a small dinner party for friends and pulled out the good china. Any time I was going to make a quiet dinner for me and my husband, I served it on the Prince Albert. Better to have dined like a queen on fine china edged with gold, than everyday ceramic plates while gazing at the china in the cabinet.

I used to own a collector car that I rarely drove. It was a 1949 Chevy Fleetline Fastback. I had sunk about $4000.00 dollars into the paint job alone. I would pass by it on my way through the garage. I would stroke the shiny glass finish on the fender and remark how beautiful she was. Then I continued walking to the driveway to get into my truck to go to work. I sold it and ended up buying a red convertible, and I drove it like I stole it.

I decided to enjoy what I had, because if I never used it and enjoyed it, it would be like I never had it. It wasn't worth having if I could only look at it. Live your life, use your china, and don't wait till it's too late, because the Pope isn't coming to dinner.

My 1949 Chevy Fleetline

Mangia! Mangia!

When my parents were growing up, both of their families were so poor that they didn't have a lot to eat. They had lived through the great depression. They both remember meager dinners at home. As economic conditions improved, food was abundant, and rarely did anyone go hungry.

When I was growing up, my mother cooked a lot of food and would bring it to the table and say Mangia! Mangia! Which means Eat! Eat! In Italian. It was an order, not a suggestion. And eat you would. It was customary to eat a lot because it was a compliment to the cook, which was usually the lady of the house. If you didn't eat much it was like saying the food was bad and it was an insult to the cook. No one ever said that you were fat or that you should quit eating and go on a diet. Never.

When I was young I remember we would have company, and it wasn't long before my mother offered our guests some coffee or other drink of their choice, and that was just to keep them occupied while she put together a small meal. If people just happened to stop by at dinner time, she would always invite them to stay for dinner because my mother cooked enough that she would always have leftovers anyway.

One day, I went to an all you can eat buffet. I ate so much that I was miserable. Afterwards, I went to visit my grandmother, Josephine. She asked me if I was hungry, and I said that I had just came from an all you can eat buffet, and I couldn't eat another bite. I had gone to the bathroom and when I came out, the table was full of food. I don't know how she came up with it all so fast. Cookies, snacks, anything she could find coupled with coffee, and tea to chase it down with. I said again that I wasn't hungry, and she replied, "Oh, you can eat some more". I'm sure she was insulted because I didn't eat a bite.

When my nephew, Paul, turned one, my husband and I went to his first birthday party. My husband and I were newlyweds, and he had not yet met my sister because she lived in Florida when we had gotten married. This would be the first time my sister had met him. I told my husband that in order to make a good impression on my sister, he had to go there really hungry, pile his plate high with a lot of food, and eat a lot. First impressions are very important.

My husband went into the kitchen and put some food on his plate, and came and sat down across from me at the picnic table. I looked at his plate and remarked about the lack of food on it. Next, my sister, Linda, comes and sits down next to him. She looks at his plate and says "is that all you're going to eat?" I looked at my husband and said, "I told you so".

Our Lady of the Snows

My mother died on February 26, 2002. I always wondered if the date had a special meaning, because sometimes I think that things can be a sign from God. Not only that, but my mother had a way about her that sometimes she would say things or know things that turned out to have a profound meaning. I did note that she died on Purim, a special Jewish holiday, where the Jews triumphed over those that wanted to kill them. But we weren't Jewish.

When the day of my mother's funeral came, there was a terrible blizzard. Because of the bad weather, there weren't a lot of people at my mom's funeral. On the way to the cemetery, after the funeral mass, the snow was so bad it was hard to see where the road was. My sister, Linda, and I were in the back of the Limo, and I looked out and saw that they were taking a remote country road to the cemetery. I was almost terrified that we wouldn't make it to the cemetery, and I wished that they would have stocked the limo with wine or champagne to calm my nerves. We finally arrived at the cemetery and the graveside formalities were kept short due to the weather. However, the blizzard on the day of my mother's funeral would come to be some sort of divine signpost to me.

My husband and I met and got married when we were both living in Rockford, Illinois. Soon after Stephen and I were married, we made a trip to Italy. I had made plans to go to Italy a long time before we had even been dating. It was one of the things on my bucket list, not just Italy, but I told God that I wanted to see Pope John Paul II before he died, or I died.

The tour group we were traveling with was one that was actually organized through the Catholic Shrine, called Our Lady of the Snows. It's located just a few miles southeast of St. Louis, Missouri, in Belleville, Illinois, near where my husband was originally from. The trip was supposed to be a catholic pilgrimage, so we also had Father Jim, our very own travelling priest with us. He would be saying mass for us every day, somewhere, or anywhere he could find to say it. He even said it when we were in the catacombs. He came completely equipped with all the mass gear one would need to say mass on the run: vestments, chalice, wafers, etc. And as for the wine, well, we were in Italy, where they use wine in place of water, so we never ran out.

This trip would also be my husband's introduction to the Catholic faith, as he was brought up Baptist. But it didn't matter, because, we were both now non denominational. I may not be a practicing Catholic every week, but I was pretty sure I could pull off reciting the mass in its entirety from rote memory, which was drilled into me by the nuns at St. Edward's School, in my early childhood. Not much had changed in the mass since they decided to say it in English, in the early "70's. It wasn't until just a few years ago, that they made some liturgical changes without consulting me first. Now when we attend an occasional mass, I am completely lost and I keep reciting the same thing I was taught as a child.

I told Steve not to tell Father Jim that he wasn't catholic. I knew the priest would cut him off from communion if he knew. Well, Steve didn't believe me, and he kept blabbing his mouth, and one day Fr. Jim told him that he couldn't give him communion anymore, and that he was cut off. Of course I had to say, "I told you so".

The first full day in Italy was a real treat for me, because we got passes to be seated in the reserved area for the pope's usual Wednesday address to the people. The moment I had thought would never happen in my life, actually became a reality. There I was, in the presence of Pope John Paul II.

After that, we toured the Vatican Museum, Tivoli Gardens, Assisi, the excavation of Pompeii, and so many other places. We visited so many churches in Italy that it was just a blur. The most memorable ones were St. Peter's Cathedral at the Vatican, and St. John the Lateran (the original Basilica). Besides these, the church that left the most lasting impression on us was the Basilica of Santa Maria Maggiore (St. Mary Major).

As legend has it, there was a devout nobleman and his wife that lived in Rome. They were very pious, but since they had no children, they wanted to dedicate all their worldly possessions to the Mother Mary. They sought direction through prayer, and one night Mother Mary appeared to both the nobleman and his wife, and also to the pope. She said she wanted the nobleman to build her a church on the top of a certain hill. She said that he would find snow in the spot where they were to build the church. The snow was to be a sign of confirmation.

On a hot August night, in 352 A.D., snow fell in Rome. In the morning, news of the summer snowfall spread. The nobleman, his wife, the pope, and the whole town flocked to the hilltop to find snow on the ground, detailing the exact shape and perimeters that they were to build the church. The pope proclaimed that the snow was from the "Queen of Heaven", and then all the people started shouting, "Our Lady of the Snows", over and over. And this was how the church got its original name of Our Lady of the Snows. They built the church, and it still stands there today, and is called the Basilica of St. Mary Major, because it is the mother of all other churches that honor the mother Mary. The Shrine in Belleville, Illinois is named after this very church that is located on a hilltop in Italy.

My husband was a company truck driver, and he drove for a company out of Rockford, Illinois. He had always wanted to own his own truck, so we were looking everywhere for a truck to buy. We looked at trucks for sale at all the dealerships in every state we would drive through, but nothing seemed to be agreeable to both of us. He was looking for a certain make, model, and drivetrain. And since I traveled with him most of the time, I wanted to make sure the bunk was to my liking. My husband was sent out to Ohio, and upstate New York on a pretty regular basis, so we spent a lot of time looking for trucks there too.

When we were in Youngstown, Ohio, we drove into this truck dealership, which did not even appear to be open.

It was a really snowy day, and the lot, and the trucks were all covered up with over a foot of snow on them. We were looking at their trucks, and they had left them all unlocked, so we climbed inside them to get a better look. We had to brush mounds of snow off the trucks to get in, or to even see what color they were.

We brushed away the snow on one of the trucks and it was a lavender or light purple color, which was one of my mother's favorite colors. I climbed inside of it, went into the bunk, and instantly fell in love with it. It had grey button and tufted interior, skylights, and a roof hatch. It had everything I wanted and more, it even had a sink!

I was standing there inside of that truck thinking this was the one I wanted to buy, this was it! I suddenly became very sad and I was almost in tears because I wanted to show this to my mom, but I couldn't because she had already passed away two years before, and I missed her greatly. As I was standing there in the bunk, I saw my mother for just a second or two. Her spirit, or her ghost, whatever you want to call it, walked through the truck. I took this as a sign that my mother approved of the truck, and God was letting me share this with my mom, even though she now resides in heaven. It took a while to cut through some red tape, but a couple months later we were the proud owners of a Purple 1999 Kenworth W900L Semi with an 86" bunk.

And so this whole series of events was how we came to refer to my mother as "Our Lady of the Snows". Now when it snows, particularly on certain days or events, I think of my mom, and I wonder if she is giving me a sign from heaven. I have also learned to pay attention to the small ways in which God tries to speak to us, each and every day.

The Tourist

I always loved to travel, and it runs in the family. My mother liked to travel, and she went around the world. My sister, Linda, is also a world traveler; only she went around it twice.

When I was single, I traveled to several continents, and took as many side trips as I could. I never passed up an opportunity for adventure, and as a result, found myself in some interesting places.

My husband is a truck driver, and when we got married, I traveled with him most of the time. Then we bought our own truck. It was lavender, and my husband, Steve, called it the lavender love shack. It had an 86 inch bunk on the back of the cab, and had almost all the comforts of home, including a T.V., VCR, refrigerator, microwave, sink, and even a porta potty. I had my laptop with wireless internet, and I even had a printer. We traveled all over the United States, from New York to California. There were only a few states that we didn't go through, which were somewhere in the north east. We would drive by landmarks and attractions, and I would say, "Hey, do we have time to stop there?"

It soon occurred to me that I could turn Steve's job into an unending paid vacation. Every time he would load for a destination, I would get on the computer to find what attractions were on the way to, or near our destination. Then I would devise a plan that would make it possible to be able to stop there. I called attractions for information, and to see if I could park a semi there. If we couldn't park there, I would a call truck stop to see if we could drop the trailer there and leave it for a while.

When we would drive through a town where a relative lived, we would call them up and arrange to meet them. We would park the truck somewhere, sometimes in a Wal-Mart parking lot, and our relatives would come pick us up to go to dinner with them. We were able to visit many relatives that we otherwise would never have been able to see. I got to visit my cousin, Anna, and her daughters in California, and my uncle, Guy, and his wife, Sandy, in Tennessee. I even got to visit my sister, Linda, and her husband, Larry, in Florida, more than once. We also got to visit with Steve's Uncle Has in Kentucky, and some of his cousins in the Northeast.

We saw everything from Niagara Falls, to the Golden Gate Bridge, and a lot of stuff in between like Wall Drug, and Mt. Rushmore. Some of my best trips were going down to Texas where we went to the Kemah Boardwalk on the ocean in Texas, the Lyndon B. Johnson Space Center, and the Alamo in San Antonio, Texas. I even got to see Moody Gardens which are located in Glass Pyramids on Galveston Island.

I collected pictures and memorabilia and made a bunch of scrapbooks full of these mementos of places we visited, and different restaurants we ate at. Every time we got within 75 miles of an ocean, I knew that I could get fresh seafood, so we were always looking for a good restaurant to eat at. We also got acquainted with some really good regular buffets that we would stop at on our way to somewhere. We liked the prime rib buffets near Las Vegas, and the seafood buffets on the east coast.

Steve said that before he married me, he would spend any free time he had at the truck stop, and didn't do a lot of venturing out. After he married me, he got to see the United States, from a tourist's point of view.

After several years we decided to move to a different state, so we sold the lavender love shack, ending our perpetual vacation. I look back on those days with fond memories, however, I don't miss the claustrophobic close quarters that the bunk of a semi provides, no matter how well equipped. I look forward to someday purchasing a real RV, so we can go on vacation in style.

Stephen and I in San Antonio

In The Balance

To help track my progress with my weight loss, or weight gain mostly, I had bought a digital scale. It was one of the first ones that came out and it wasn't very accurate. There was this dial on the bottom where you could adjust it to try and get it to go to zero as a starting weight. Two pounds was as low as the setting would go, however you could add up to about 20lbs. on to it if you wanted to. The instructions said to step on the scale three times and then average the weights together. I got in the habit of stepping on it, and then getting off, and repeating this several times each morning, in hopes that I would get lighter each time I stepped on it.

My skinny husband started stepping on the scale to watch his weight, or to check the pressure in his spare tire, I'm not sure which. I found it amusing because every time I go on a major diet, he loses 10 pounds in a month, and I lose, maybe 3. Not fair. So knowing that he was going to step on the scale Saturday morning, I turned the dial up 10 pounds. He stepped on the scale and was so shocked that he had put on 10 pounds. I was standing behind him, trying to exercise so much self-control so as not to fall over laughing, that I almost got stomach cramps. He got off the scale and I adjusted my face to look almost concerned, squeezing the muscles on the sides of my cheeks to prevent a grin from forming. "Well honey", I said, "You're going to have to lay off all that junk food, and French fries". I couldn't believe he didn't catch on as it was all I could do to act normal.

Several days went by and I adjusted the setting on the scale down by 5 pounds. He was so happy to have lost five pounds so quickly. I commended him for such a good job. I was happy to have my little prank go as well as I don't have much to do in this small town we live in, and conducting experiments on my husband is one of the few entertaining pastimes I have.

My scale was so discouragingly inaccurate that I decided I needed to buy a better one. I was at Aldi one day when I spotted a digital scale. It was after News Year's day, when everyone in the whole world starts their diet to lose all the holiday pounds they put on. I put it in my cart. I didn't pay a lot for it, but I was still hopeful that it would be a big improvement over my last scale.

When I got home, I opened the box, removed the contents, and read the directions. It said the scale would calculate your BMI; tell you what your body water ratio was, and how many calories you should consume every day. I was excited to get an accurate scale that had all these extra features on it. Per the directions, in order to set it up to display all this data, I had to enter my age, and target weight, and then step on it. When I stepped on it, it said "ERROR". So I picked up the directions and read the error codes in the troubleshooting section. It said that my body weight was outside of measurable limits. I was upset that my new scale had been programmed for a supermodel stick figure.

"I'M NOT THAT FAT!" I yelled at the scale.

My new scale had deemed me too obese to calculate all the fancy data. It would display my weight if I just stepped on it, but would not do all the things it boasted about doing on the front of the box and in the directions. It worked great for my skinny husband though. It gave him his BMI, body water ratio, his target weight, and how many calories he should be consuming each day. My new scale was a traitor.

One day when my husband stepped on the new scale, I was thinking that I could not play the same trick on him as before, because there was no dial adjustment on this one. But I decided I would stick my toe on the back edge of it, as I was standing behind him a couple feet away. So I stretched my leg out and put my toe on the back edge of the scale. I tried to just put a little pressure on the edge of it to add only about 10 pounds. Instead of 10 lbs., it was more like 20. He was raising his voice. "That's not right", he said as he got off the scale and then stepped right back on. Again I put my toe on the back edge of the scale, amazed that he didn't or couldn't see my toe on the back edge of the scale. Again I had put too much weight on it, and it gave such an off target reading, he turned to me and said, "Ok, what did you do to the scale?"

How to Say "I Like You" in Italian

When I was growing up, my mother would occasionally pinch my butt. I learned it was a sign of affection. Occasionally, I would get an affectionate slap on the butt. For Italians, it's not always a sexual gesture, like it is here in America. However, neither my father nor my brother pinched my but, because that would have been inappropriate. Apparently mothers have a license to pinch their children's butts.

When my son, Anthony, was born, he was the most beautiful baby. Every time I would change his diaper, it was hard to resist pinching his butt. And so there began a lifetime of butt pinching for him. When I talk to him on the phone, I tell him to pinch his own butt for me. The last few times we saw each other, he has pinched my butt before I could pinch his. When I remarried, my son pinched my husband's butt. I told my husband, Steve, that's how he could tell my son liked him. My son has a friend that is also Italian, and when he was growing up, his mother pinched his butt also.

I unconsciously pinched a man's butt once in Hawaii. He had a British accent, and he was my dive instructor. He wasn't like Johnny Depp, or Brad Pitt handsome, or even sexy, but I just liked him. As he walked by, I reached out and pinched his butt. I was almost as shocked as he was. I really didn't mean to flirt with him, I was just used to doing that to people I liked.

One time my mother went to Italy, and a man actually asked for her permission to pinch her butt. She was probably in her sixties. It would have been a compliment, but she declined the proposition as she was a married woman.

I knew a man once that was always playing practical jokes on everyone, including me. His wife pinched my butt just to drive her husband crazy, because he was so uptight about it. It would have been inappropriate for me to pinch his butt, so I asked my husband to pinch his butt for me. Needless to say the guy lost it, however, his wife found it hilarious.

Don't try this on just anyone, particularly in the U.S, you might get slapped or maybe even arrested. Try it with your significant other, it will give a new meaning to reach out and touch someone.

Milton Keynes UK
Ingram Content Group UK Ltd.
UKHW021824041023
429927UK00014B/443